Unlimited

KNOWING OUR IDENTITY
AND FINDING OUR PURPOSE
A devotional journey

Copyright © Jen Baker, 2014

Published 2015 by CWR, Waverley Abbey House, Waverley Lane, Farnham, Surrey GU9 8EP, UK. Registered Charity No. 294387. Registered Limited Company No. 1990308.

Paperback edition published 2019.

The right of Jen Baker to be identified as the author of this work has been asserted by her in accordance with the Copyright, Designs and Patents Act 1988, sections 77 and 78.

Author photograph © Claire Parkinson at Navy Frame.

For a list of National Distributors go to cwr.org.uk/distributors

Unless otherwise indicated, all Scripture references are from THE HOLY BIBLE, NEW INTERNATIONAL VERSION®, NIV®, copyright © 1973, 1978, 1984, 2011 by Biblica Inc. Used by permission. All rights reserved.

Other Scripture quotations are marked: Amplified: Scripture taken from the Amplified® Bible, copyright © 1954, 1958, 1964, 1965, 1987 by The Lockman Foundation. Used by permission. ERV: The Easy-To-Read Version, copyright © 2006 by World Bible Translation Center. ESV: Scripture taken from the ESV® Bible (The Holy Bible, English Standard Version®), copyright © 2001 by Crossway, a publishing ministry of Good News Publishers. Used by permission. All rights reserved. NASB: Scripture taken from the NEW AMERICAN STANDARD BIBLE®, copyright © 1960, 1962, 1963, 1968, 1971, 1972, 1973, 1975, 1977, 1995 by The Lockman Foundation. Used by permission. NKJV: Scripture taken from the New King James Version®, copyright © 1982 by Thomas Nelson. Used by permission. All rights reserved. The Message: Scripture taken from The Message, copyright © 1993, 1994, 1995, 1996, 2000, 2001, 2002. Used by permission of NavPress Publishing Group.

Every effort has been made to ensure that this book contains the correct permissions and references, but if anything has been inadvertently overlooked the Publisher will be pleased to make the necessary arrangements at the first opportunity. Please contact the Publisher directly.

Concept development, editing, design and production by CWR.

Printed in the UK by Page Bros

ISBN: 978-1-78951-259-5

Contents

Introduction

Welcome to a twelve-week journey, created to demystify purpose and reveal your unlimited potential. I'm so pleased you have picked up this book and I trust God will speak to you powerfully over this next season!

I often hear young ladies speak of not knowing their purpose, and have seen older women go to their graves carrying the baggage of 'what if' and regret. I am passionate about inspiring others to live a full life – their *intended* life. And that passion is what inspired me to write this book, believing this will help you live a life of great adventure; the one for which we have all been created!

During my first year at university (Hope College in Holland, Michigan) I was a theatre major, and I vividly remember one class where they taught us how to walk. Whilst you would think every university student should already have that simple act mastered, we were amazed at how much there was to learn!

The professor explained that we all *lead* from one particular part of our body. It's subtle, but it is there. Some may lead with their chins, others by their knees, others by their waist – but there is one part which draws us forward, and if that part changes, so does our walk.

In *Unlimited*, we explore four ways in which our body leads us, and as we study them, we will have opportunity to strengthen each.

As each part grows stronger, the body will inevitably change its 'walk'… our head will be held higher, steps planted firmer, and our purpose will become clearer.

The four ways are simply:

Voice – *Who you are*
Hands – *What you are*
Heart – *Why you are*
Feet – *Where you are*

These sections make up the four parts of this book. Each part in turn covers three weekly devotionals focusing on that particular theme, leading you towards a greater understanding of purpose, identity and influence.

I pray the Holy Spirit blesses your time in this book with revelation, peace, grace, confidence and direction.

You are beautiful.
Your future is powerful.
Enjoy the journey.

THANK YOU

In actual fact, a book is written by a team, never an author.

Thank you CWR for approaching me to write this second book – your support and staff have always made the experience a pleasure! I especially want to thank Lynette Brooks for your guidance, Lauren Darby for being such a fab and fun editor and Ben Knight for your excellent design support.

Thank you to my faithful friends supporting me in prayer over the years. Specifically Amber, Christy, Kay, Chris, Kerry, Tanja, Beth, Phil, my Prayer Team, and the *countless* others who cheer me on!

Thank you Lisa M for assembling the table.

Thank you Lisa D for supporting me behind the scenes with such excellence.

Thank you Bev Murrill for publishing my first article and believing in me as a writer.

Thank you Elaine Miller for mentoring me for the past sixteen years; I honour you and will miss you deeply. I look forward to sipping tea with you again one day...

Thank you to Hope City Church, especially Dave and Jen Gilpin, who selflessly encourage the dreams of countless thousands – myself included.

Thank you to my family in the US and my 'family' in the UK – I love you.

Thank you Mom for the thousands of prayers you have prayed for me.

Thank You to my heavenly Father, my Best Friend, the One who gives me breath, and the One who will forever hold my awe... I love You so very much.

And finally...

I dedicate this book to my father – Robert Baker. A man who lives with passion, purpose, direction and devotion. My desire to live a full life, never giving up, always persevering, comes directly from seeing it modelled for me as a child, through you. I love you. Isaiah 40:29–31.

Aside from French foodies, who really appreciates a creature that takes five hours to walk an inch? #boring

And finally – the ultimate...

Spiders.

I have no words.

Why God Almighty created spiders is beyond me. I don't even like typing the word – it makes my skin crawl. No pun intended.

Just this evening I was sitting in a hotel lobby having a drink with a friend, when out of nowhere, I saw one of... 'those'... dangling in midair.

MIDAIR.

Like an abseiler looking for his mountain.

Screaming, I point, but of course my friend couldn't see him because he was in the air.

'The clock?'

'NO.'

'The door?'

'NO!'

'It's a sssspppiiiiddddeerrrrr!' I screamed, whilst curled up in a ball on the sofa.

Yeah, I know, drama queen.

It took no imagination at all to imagine myself grabbing the nearest bloke and arm wrestling him into the room to save us.

The abseiler was the size of my thumb, but in my mind – I was no match for him.

Fear had overtaken reality. Therefore, *fear had become reality.*

We are created for faith, not fear.

And as long as we let fear win – faith will stay in his corner, typing on his smartphone, waiting to be called into the game.

So, want to know something ironic? I was typing this devotional in room 360 of my hotel, and as I got to that last part about faith, guess what I caught out of the corner of my eye?

Yep.

The little abseiler had crawled up three flights of stairs, found my room, and was *running across my floor.*

(We interrupt this devotion so I can jump onto the bed.)

He is now sitting five feet from me – under a glass.

At this exact moment I have a choice to make – faith or fear?

So do you...

My room number was 360 – an appropriate number for the beginning of a devotional that will encourage a 360-degree look at life! Declare your intention to be REAL with the Lord over the next twelve weeks. To be honest. To listen. To DREAM.

What shouts loudest is usually heard. Would you say faith or fear screams the loudest in your life at the moment? Or in which area(s) does fear have the upper hand? Take a few minutes to look fear in the eye, and then deliberately decide it will not stop you from progressing these next twelve weeks. Faith is now your faithful companion, and strongest advocate on this journey...

Tuesday

W e start this section looking at our voice. Not literally, as that would be weird, but figuratively discovering another inflection to the sound we have been born to share.

A sound that is unique. A sound all our own. A sound that won't be heard if we do not have the courage to speak.

One greatly misunderstood piece of Scripture is 1 Corinthians 14:34–35, where the apostle Paul asks women to be silent, and to gain their learning at home. He wasn't against women learning or having a voice, he was addressing a specific situation and we mustn't take this out of context or use it literally today.

You are not meant to be silent; you are meant to have a voice.

And that voice is meant to change your world.

Who currently in your world can you influence without words, by living a life fully sold out to God's purpose?

Think about those nearby and those further away,
who you could influence with your voice (eg family
members, work colleagues, neighbours, people as you
travel, work colleagues in other cities, mums at school,
teachers, health staff etc). List the names of those you
particularly want to help or encourage with your words.

Steve, Grace, Alice, Lily, Ma,
Charlotte, Helen, Alice F, Nadine,
Taryn, Meg

The term 'influence' is defined as:

A. The capacity or power of persons or things to be a
compelling force on or produce effects on the actions,
behaviour, opinions etc of others.

B. The action or process of producing effects on the actions,
behaviour, opinions etc of another or others.

These definitions explain the force behind influence, as both
capacity *and* process. We all have the capacity to affect another
person or society, but we must realise this is a process and also
involves intentionality.

We are going to explore this a bit more in the next few days,
but for today ask God to begin expanding your influence. Ask
Him to show you where your greatest influence lies at the
moment.

And ask Him for courage to speak...

Wednesday

As we saw yesterday, one of the definitions for influence is:

The capacity or power of persons or things to be a compelling force on or produce effects on the actions, behaviour, opinions, etc of others.

You have the capacity to bring change. More than that
– you were born to affect change.

If you doubt that, look at a baby. Even a tiny child, helpless to do anything, can influence change using his voice. One little cry and he gets fed, his nappy gets changed and a cuddle is on the horizon.

With maturity, the whining becomes authority. *We no longer 'cry' to get attention, we speak to give direction.*

Think for a minute – do you find yourself seeking attention rather than direction? How, when and with whom is it most tempting?

Only from Steve, decision making. I fear the repercussion of making the wrong one as Steve always has an opinion

In which areas are you most tempted to revert to 'childlike' behaviour? For example, sulking, complaining, whingeing, backbiting...

when talking with close
Friends - Alice F, Jackie but
whinging about others.

We often hurt those closest to us through our childlike behaviour. Ask the Holy Spirit to show you if there is anyone you need to apologise to or seek forgiveness from, due to your recent behaviour?

If anyone comes to mind, act quickly and apologise as soon as possible.

Silence (Tyler Staiton)
2 Tim 1:7
Life is too momentary to be timid!

Thursday

T he other definition for influence, which we read on Tuesday, said:

The action or process of producing effects on the actions, behaviour, opinions etc of another or others.

We have the ability to affect the actions of others. And if you doubt that, remember the infant. Babies change the world of their parents, from the moment of birth. Suddenly normal, intelligent, potentially reserved adults begin making unintelligent noises, strange faces and can start acting like children themselves!

How many times have you been walking down the street and have seen someone coming in the other direction toward you? More often than not, as you slightly lean to one side of the pavement, they move to the other side, as there is an unspoken understanding of who will pass on which side of the pavement.

What are some ways, subtle or otherwise, in which you intentionally influence people in your day-to-day life?

1-1s, hub, open space, Encounter, Family life.

Influence. Subtle, yet real.

With action must come intent. And with intention comes commitment. Otherwise relationships will be rife with misunderstanding and hurt. In Matthew 28:18–19 (Amplified) it says:

'Jesus approached and, breaking the silence, said to them, All authority (all power of rule) in heaven and on earth has been given to Me. Go then and make disciples of all the nations, baptizing them into the name of the Father and of the Son and of the Holy Spirit'

Are you willing to break your silence, and commit to the influence (discipling) of others?

Friday

A t the beginning of this week we read that each of us has a unique sound. A sound meant to influence. A sound meant to evoke change, encourage hope and establish peace in the lives of those around us. A sound unique to our calling and our place at this moment in history. A sound of freedom.

Psalm 27:1 says 'The LORD is my light and my salvation – whom shall I fear? The LORD is the stronghold of my life – of whom shall I be afraid?'

And in Isaiah 41:13 it says 'For I am the LORD your God who takes hold of your right hand and says to you, Do not fear; I will help you.'

My fear of spiders is significant, but at the end of the day let's be honest – unless I'm called to be a missionary in Africa (which currently I am not), it isn't going to affect my long-term purpose too much.

But the fear of man – will.

And if we allow the fear of man to override our fear of God, the future He has for us will be hampered and the plans He desires for us may be missed.

The consequence isn't lack of God's love, it is loss of full impact.

Read the previous two pieces of Scripture again. And again.
Out loud.

Then declare the following:

Lord, I thank You for Your love for me. Thank You that You made me
unique and You gave me a voice. This voice is meant to impact and
influence my world. I declare that fear is not my master. I declare
that You are with me. I declare the past is not my future. I declare
that even if it's shaking, I will use my voice to speak Your words with
no compromise. I declare I will speak grace-filled words of truth,
hope, peace and love to a world desperately in need of a Saviour.
Thank You for being with me and giving me the words to say. I love
You. Amen.

Monday

It doesn't take a rocket scientist to work a kettle.

'Therefore, if anyone is in Christ, the new creation has come: The old has gone, the new is here!' (2 Cor. 5:17)

S o when I was visiting a poorly friend at her house and she requested a cup of tea, I assumed it was within my skill set.

Walking into the kitchen I perused my surroundings. Kettle on hob. Sink to the left. Milk in the fridge. Teabags in the tin. Let's go.

I filled the kettle up with water, returned it to the hob, and turned the knob to medium.

Then I waited.

And waited.

And… nothing.

Thinking the hob wasn't working right, I turned the knob to the highest number. I hate to wait on the best of days, but especially when a cup of tea or coffee is involved.

I soon discovered the proverb was right – a watched pot never boils.

After approximately two minutes of delay and frustration, with no boil, I picked up the kettle to check the hob.

And as it turned out… this kettle was electric.

What I now held in my hand was a kettle and hob kissing, via the melted rubber attached to both the underside of the kettle and the top of the burner.

My unwell friend had left the kettle on the hob because she was ill, and it was easier to leave it there than put it where it belonged.

This was an *electric* kettle, which would excel and produce at its highest capacity when connected in the appropriate way. Labelling it a stove-top kettle, would never change its purpose or function.

Likewise with us.

If we allow others to label us as something that we aren't,
our purpose won't change, but the outcome might.

In addition to the powerful truth quoted at the beginning about being new, God also says we are conquerors (Rom. 8:37). *Believing* these truths connects us to our purpose.

As we stay connected spiritually to the Word and by the Spirit, our future productivity and influence grows.

So, make a cuppa, take a few minutes to check your connection, let the truth of those scriptures speak to you as you spend five minutes meditating on them, and prepare this week to hear His voice of grace and truth...

Tuesday

Whether we like it or not, labels make a difference. They define. They explain. They isolate.

Prada is different to Primark. That's not a judgment, it's a fact. The material is different, the feel is different, and at a closer look, the quality is different.

But it does not make the Primark wearer any more or less qualified than the Prada wearer. The label doesn't equip the person any more than carrying a smartphone makes you an IT wizard. It is simply a label.

This week, let's take some time to explore labels – the good, bad, and yes – even some ugly ones.

As mentioned yesterday, the Bible says, 'Therefore, if anyone is in Christ, he is a new creation. The old has passed away; behold, the new has come.' (2 Cor. 5:17, ESV).

When we become Christians, we don't get a new label, we have a new *identity*.

Nevertheless, many do see Christianity as a label, not an identity. It is used to describe who we are, what we believe and how we view the world around us.

But identity goes much deeper than this. *At the core of our being, we have been changed.* Not for a fad and not for a season, but for eternity…

What types of labels have others put on you over the years that you need to choose to FORGET?

....

....

....

What types of labels have you given yourself?

....

....

....

What type of label would you *like* to wear? For example, overcomer, blessed, highly favoured, generous, life-giving, inspirational, kind, empowering…

....

....

....

....

Write your favourite label on a sticky note and put it somewhere you will see every day. When you are tempted to think of yourself differently, declare these truths over yourself. Be intentional about this!

Wednesday

In Matthew 16, Jesus asks His disciples who people say that He is. Peter answers by saying, 'You are the Messiah, the Son of the living God' (v16).

Jesus asked who people thought He was, not because He questioned His identity, but because He desired their revelation.

If anyone knew their identity, it was Jesus. He later said that He only ever came to do what His Father asked Him to do (John 6:38), only to say what His Father asked Him to say (John 12:49) and that His job description involved seeking and saving those who were lost (Luke 19:10).

He knew why He was here, who He should listen to and what He should say. There was no confusion.

Our confusion comes when we cannot answer those questions: Why am I here? Who is my authority? How shall I respond?

Without clear direction to those questions, we open ourselves up to vast amounts of confusion and identity crises. Decisions are made about our future that we may not agree with, but feel we have no other choice but to follow. Our responses come from the media or what is popular, versus our convictions. We hesitate to disagree with anyone, based on our desire to please and insecurity around confrontation.

Knowing our identity is crucial to owning our future.

If you struggle in this area, take some time to pray about it and think about how you submit to God's authority, what that looks like and whether it feels empowering or controlling.

In actuality, proper submission is always empowering, never controlling.

Dear Father, thank You for how You see me. I'm Your much loved and much wanted daughter. Knowing You has changed my future and knowing how You see me can change my present. Thank You that You empower, but never control. Remove wrong mindsets and open my eyes to the truth. Please reveal to me this week any incorrect labels and help me in turn apply Your Word to my identity. Thank You. Amen.

Thursday

Part of knowing who we are, is knowing who we aren't. Knowing what you *don't* want to be or where you *don't* want to end up, helps define who you can be and the direction you prefer to be moving in.

In John 6:60–69 it says that many people left Jesus because His teaching was too hard. He looked at His disciples and asked them if they were also going to leave, but they said they had nowhere else to go. They weren't sure where following Him would take them, but they were sure that *not* following Him would deter them from what they truly desired.

It is still the same today.

Following Him may be confusing at times and lack of certainty about our future plans will be the hallmark of most days. But *not* following Him will *always* lack direction and leave us feeling void of purpose and legacy.

But *not* following Him will *always* lack direction, leaving us feeling void of purpose and lacking in legacy. For many legacies are birthed out of purpose lived. In fact, I would suggest *real identity always leaves the footprint of legacy behind*, because purpose fulfilled cannot help but leave an impression.

What is your greatest fear – if you have one – about completely surrendering to the plans and purposes of God?

. . . .

. . . .

. . . .

. . . .

Is there anything at all that you hold in the 'don't go there, God' box? (Please, be honest.)

. . . .

. . . .

. . . .

. . . .

Could you trust God to do what's necessary to bring you freedom? Journal your thoughts.

. . . .

. . . .

. . . .

. . . .

Friday

Having clarity around our identity opens the door to our destiny. It sounds a bit like bravado, but it is true.

Without knowing our identity, we spend much of our lives searching out who we are and why we are here. Many people go to their graves still not knowing why they lived. That to me is one of the greatest tragedies of our time and part of the reason why I wanted to write this book. In today's society, more than ever, we get caught in the 'now' instead of the 'not yet'.

If we allow greed, lust, advancement and status to entrap us, we will forsake a future of blessings, promotion, purity and wealth found in God's timing.

In your life, where have you been most tempted to the 'now' as opposed to the 'not yet'? For example, a new car, marriage, children, career advancement, designer clothes, chocolate (sorry, girls!)... the list truly is endless!

Remember that just desiring something will not make a difference – your want must be intentional, and directional.

In other words, what you desire to achieve must be greater than what currently tempts you.

Record here what dreams it would be worth overcoming those temptations to achieve (eg having fruitful and blessed relationships, fulfilling God's will for you in your workplace... You can be more specific).

. . . .

. . . .

. . . .

Be honest – REALLY honest – *do you want to change?*

If the answer to that is yes, then write here what you will do practically to make that happen. Some suggestions: start saving money, refuse to buy impulsively, go to bed earlier, have regular quiet times, read books that are positive and life-giving.

. . . .

. . . .

Finally, who can hold you accountable to this? Find someone you trust who will *really* hold you accountable to these changes – someone who will encourage you and will always tell the truth. Then write in your calendar every day what you plan to do – for the next thirty days. In thirty days from now you will be asked in this book how you did, so be ready to write a praise report!

Monday

One teaspoon of baking soda.

'In a word, what I'm saying is, *Grow up*. You're kingdom subjects. Now live like it. Live out your God-created identity. Live generously and graciously toward others, the way God lives toward you.'

(Matt. 5:48, *The Message*)

WEEK 3: THE MISSING INGREDIENT

P eriodically I get sudden urges to bake.

I say periodically because I live alone and have a hectic schedule, which drastically reduces the ability, and desire, to create masterpieces in the kitchen on a regular basis.

But on this particular day I had the time, inclination, and mushy bananas, to make this impulse a reality – freshly baked banana bread was on the cards.

Putting on worship music, donning my favourite cooking apron and getting out the ingredients, had me stirring, mixing and preparing in no time. All done, I stuck it in the oven and busied myself with other activities as I waited.

Hearing the timer, I rushed to see my creation in all its glory; only to realise it was much less glorious than I had planned.

My bread was flat, not fluffy.

It was then I remembered the baking soda. My first thought was, 'I guess they really meant what they said when the recipe asked for baking soda.'

It's like God – He means what He says.

When He says that He forgives us, He does. When He says that He loves you, He does. When He says to love your neighbour – He means it.

Words have power and our voices are meant to carry authority.

If you doubt that, remind yourself that you are created in God's image. And when His voice was used, the world as we know it was formed (see Gen. 1).

Therefore, if we are made in His image, our voice carries an authority and power that most of us do not realise we possess and even fewer of us actually use.

It's time we add the ingredient of intentionality! Courageously say what we mean, and mean what we say.

'so is my word that goes out from my mouth: It will not return to me empty, but will accomplish what I desire and achieve the purpose for which I sent it.' (Isa. 55:11)

Spend a few minutes thinking about someone in your life who spoke words of encouragement over you. What did they say? How did it help you? One practical suggestion is to have a box of encouragement – it is a special box where you keep all written notes of encouragement you have received. When you are feeling fed up or downhearted – pull it out and read. If you haven't done that yet, create or buy that special box this week...

Tuesday

Hearing God's voice is crucial to correctly using our own. By not hearing God's voice we tune in to other voices, who may not have our best interest at heart.

So, how do you hear the voice of God?

Whole books have been written on this subject, so here we will simply scratch the surface. But in doing so, my desire is that *your* desire will unfold like a flower, desiring the water of His Word and warmth of His tone more than ever before.

Even as I type this, I sense the Holy Spirit. He is here. He desires to speak to you. He wants you to know God's tremendous love for you… heart toward you… yearning to have conversation with you… and genuine care for what concerns you today.

Prepare to hear His voice.

Believe that He will speak.

And He will.

One of the most famous scriptures about hearing God's voice is found in Isaiah 30:18–21.

Paraphrased and with added emphasis, it says this:

'The Lord is waiting to show His mercy to you. He wants to rise and comfort you. The Lord is the God who does the right thing, so He will bless everyone who waits for His help. You people who live in Jerusalem on Mount Zion will not continue crying. The Lord will hear your crying, and He will comfort you. When He hears you, He will help you. The Lord might give you sorrow and pain like the bread and water you eat every day, but God is your Teacher, and He will not continue to hide from you. You will see your Teacher with your own eyes. *If you wander from the right path, either to the right or to the left, you will hear a voice behind you saying, 'You should go this way. Here is the right way.'*

We hear Him more often than we realise. Not in a big booming voice, but in the still small tones of grace, forgiveness, kindness, blessings, surprises, love, gentleness, strength – all woven together throughout the tapestry of our day.

Look for Him – you *will* find Him, looking at you with such tremendous eyes of love. Waiting and ready to share your day, your laughter, your tears, your fears and your victories.

Take some time to thank Him for His presence – *and presentness* – with you now. Use this space to jot down anything you may hear Him saying to you.

Wednesday

If you are breathing, you have purpose.
And if you have purpose, you have something to say.

And with those words, you affect change.

This world needs more women walking in purpose and speaking with authority. For too many years we have been hushed, with too few willing to break the mould… and the silence. Tradition has held us back and if we dared step forward, fear would give us a warning look which had us rapidly retreating to a safer place.

Stepping out and speaking up seemed too hard for many, therefore holding our opinion and remaining calm became the acceptable norm.

Now before you get nervous, I am *not* advocating a liberal feminist movement, unsubmissive rhetoric, rude dialogue or vicious opinions.

Words must rise out of a godly spirit, not an embittered agenda.

But… words *must* rise up.

I am speaking directly to someone right now, who knows that they are not fully utilising their God-given authority. God has more for you than you are currently seeing and in your core you know it.

How much time needs to pass before you face this fear and move this mountain?

If you could have a voice about something, what would it say?

. . . .

. . . .

. . . .

. . . .

Which injustice appalls you, sorrow moves you, dream entices you or vision empowers you?

. . . .

. . . .

. . . .

. . . .

Go and tell someone. Verbalise it. And begin asking God what His next step is for you in this particular area.

Once you feel a spark of something in your spirit, you need to move on it.

Verbally.

Thursday

Our words change outcomes.

Articulating what we expect and want to see increases our faith, annoys the enemy and impacts the atmosphere. I don't honestly understand how it all works, I just know that it does.

Now of course, ultimately God is in control of our lives. I'm not advocating telling Him what to do, definitely not! But He partners with us, and He loves to see our faith in action as we speak forth what He has put in our hearts.

Jesus spoke and the centurion's servant was healed (Matt. 8:13) and in Psalm 107:20 it says 'He sent out his word and healed them'.

Word – declaration – result.

What declarations can you make today? Perhaps it's declaring God's healing touch on a family member, His salvation over a city, or His purposes to be revealed in your life.

Whatever it is, begin declaring – and believing – that your words carry authority. And as they are mixed with the power of the Spirit and truth of His Word, mountains can be moved and nations can be changed.

Father God, I declare today that there is power in Your Word.
I declare my ability to work with You, proclaiming the truth of
what You have spoken over me. I am Your chosen daughter – royal,
blessed and highly favoured. I have authority over the enemy
because of the blood of Jesus and I take captive every thought to
make it obedient to Christ. I will not shy away from Your calling,
nor will I retreat when I should advance. My voice will be grace-filled,
yet simultaneously carry power to speak what I want to see, which is
Your kingdom come and Your will be done on earth as it is in heaven.
This I will declare! Amen.

Friday

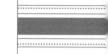

'Truly I tell you, if you have faith as small as a mustard seed, you can say to this mountain, "Move from here to there," and it will move. Nothing will be impossible for you' (Matt. 17:20).

Nothing. Will. Be. Impossible. For. YOU.

Faith + Voice = Possibility.

I often say, 'We must raise our faith to the level of His power, not lower His power to the level of our experience.' And this holds deeply true when it comes to our words.

Are your words positive or negative? Life-giving or fear-enhancing?

....

....

....

....

Let's continue this journey in regularly declaring what we want to see. Declare the best is yet to come, your future is greater than your past, God is for you, favour precedes you and blessings are coming to you. Every one of those declarations is scriptural. Therefore, each one is available for you to speak over your life.

Write out your own personal declaration here – it can be as short or as long as you want it to be (use extra paper if necessary). But make it *personal*, make it *powerful* and make it *scriptural*.

....

....

....

....

Spend time over the weekend listening to your words, and seeing how many of them are negative and how many are positive. If it helps, put up sticky notes around your house reminding you to speak LIFE into the atmosphere, keeping an attitude of thankfulness and a spirit of generosity.

Notes

Part 2

Hands

WHAT YOU ARE

'Trust in the LORD with all your heart and lean
not on your own understanding;
in all your ways submit to him, and he will
make your paths straight.' (Prov. 3:5–6)

Monday

God bless the bloodline of the man who invented the shower!

I can't tell you the number of times I have muttered those words early in the morning or after a particularly long, hot run.

Stepping into a steaming hot shower, letting the cares of the world wash away, is almost as nice as drinking a Starbucks.

Yet how many of us know the name William Feetham?

Neither did I.

In 1767 he invented the first modern-day shower. It was nothing like we enjoy today and only allowed cold, recycled, water (let's give a resounding cheer for modern technology), but it started the process of what hundreds of thousands of people enjoy today.

Prior to this, it was ice bucket washing or once-a-month baths for many people.

William could see beyond the present inconvenience, toward the not yet experienced ease of cleanliness.

Mary Shelley has written in the introduction to *Frankenstein*: 'Invention, it must be humbly admitted, does not consist in creating out of void, but out of chaos.'

What inconvenience, or chaos, today is preparing you for promotion tomorrow? We are 'inconvenienced' by bad health, unexpected bills, a wayward child, a distant husband, a frustrating boss, or a reoccurring fear. It's tempting to feel this inconvenience is here to stay and there is nothing to change our 'lot in life'.

Note here any such 'obstacles' that you think may be standing in your way at the moment:

....

....

....

....

Remember God is the God of the new; He is the God of invention. Genesis 1:1 says 'In the beginning *God created* the heavens and the earth' (emphasis mine).

He created the most beauty out of the greatest void. 'Now the earth was formless and empty, darkness was over the surface of the deep, and the Spirit of God was hovering over the waters.' (Gen. 1:2)

Trust that God is hovering in your void and around your chaos.

You are not alone. He is asking that you see the present, but also envision the future. This is not forever. You are not stuck. Hope is found in creating a new tomorrow. Mr Feetham took a step forward, which paved the way for what we enjoy today. Each step you take will pave the way for a new future to unfold.

> 'I know what I'm doing. I have it all planned out — plans to take care of you, not abandon you, plans to give you the future you hope for.' (Jer. 29:11, *The Message*)

Take five minutes to still yourself before God. Just REST. Breathe in His grace. Allow Him to declare 'peace be still' over your chaos. See the waves returning to calm, and the storm clouds moving away. Let that picture stay with you today. Allow yourself time to believe it can happen, even if you don't know how He is going to do it. He is God. He is capable.

Tuesday

Your uniqueness is released in your creativity; your creativity is found within your uniqueness.

There has never been, and will never be, another you. EVER.

Amongst other reasons, that is why the way you live your life is so important. You have a unique role to fill, an uncontested path to journey. It is yours, and only yours.

Do you believe that?

. . . .

. . . .

Before we go any further this week, the thought that you are a unique one-off *must* become ingrained in your conscience and embedded into your beliefs. For only by knowing we have purpose will we push through all that life throws at us, into all that we have been created to contribute.

Father, thank You for creating me as a 'one of a kind', with a 'one of a kind' mission to my life. I desire to embrace all that You have for me, leaving nothing left undone. Will You help me do this? You are the Redeemer of time and Giver of gifts. Use the gifts You have given me to bless those around me – bringing glory to Your name and helping many come to know You. Amen.

Journal here your thoughts on your uniqueness – what is God saying to you about this?

....

....

....

....

List out the gifts you have to contribute to the benefit of others and the glory of God.

....

....

....

....

Wednesday

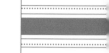

What makes your heart beat?

No, besides Mr Darcy!

What cause, activity, thought, or dream is one that would cause you to wake up in the morning with excitement in your spirit and a smile on your face?

For some, it is working with the homeless, for others it is starting a business. Maybe for you it is leading a Bible study, serving on a board or helping your daughter prepare for a spelling test?

We pass through unique seasons on this journey of life – some more hidden than others, but none less important. They all weave together into the tapestry of our lives, the picture which is played and remembered once we have breathed our final breath and our memory is rehearsed amongst others.

So, I ask again: *what makes your heart beat? And what are you doing about it?*

List your passions/dreams here – especially those unfulfilled and those that seem impossible:

. . . .

. . . .

. . . .

. . . .

Now pray for these, giving them over to God. Ask and wait for Him to show you the next practical step you should take in seeing these dreams fulfilled – however small that step may be. Perhaps memorise Psalm 37:4 this week.

Thursday

E sther was born for 'such a time as this' – many of us have heard and read that phrase before (Esth. 4:14). The Jewish people were on the edge of being annihilated and a young teenage girl was given the responsibility of halting the horror. A big calling for a little girl.

David was the ignored brother, the one left out in the fields alone with the sheep. Left alone to worship and do battle… which prepared him for escaping obscurity and leading a nation.

And then there was Edward Kimball. Not a particularly well-known name, just a simple Sunday school teacher... who led D.L. Moody to the Lord.

It's been said about Mr Moody:

'No one this side of Heaven can ever estimate the number of people he won to Christ in his evangelistic services. It has been estimated that he preached to millions. It is safe to say that he must, under the power of God, have led hundreds of thousands to a decision.'*

Hundreds of thousands were saved, because one man had a burden for souls and volunteered to teach at a Sunday school.

We do not always choose the opportunities that come our way, but we do choose our response. And we choose the level of eagerness with which we seek open doors.

Someone needs you. They need your voice, your hands, your encouragement, your talents, and your vision. You too have been born for this time. You also have the opportunity to worship in the lonely seasons. And finally, you, as well as anyone else, can step into an obscure role to make a monumental impact. You have a key part to play in humanity today – are you playing it?

All it takes is saying 'yes'.

On Tuesday we explored the unique gifts that God has given you. If you still can't think of them, ask the Holy Spirit to whisper them to you now...

And if you are still struggling, after spending time listening and praying, then ask a few trusted friends what they believe is your unique contribution in this season of life.

Trust me beloved – *you have one.*

*www.biblebelievers.com/moody/19.html

Friday

L et's finish this week with a simple, yet profound question. *God, what would You like me to be doing?*

As previously said, if we are breathing, we have purpose. If you are breathing, then there is a reason why you woke up this morning. God has plans for you.

Write down any plans, large or small, that God might be currently whispering into your heart.

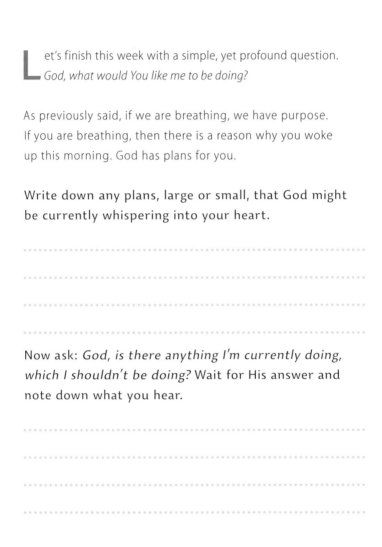

Now ask: *God, is there anything I'm currently doing, which I shouldn't be doing?* Wait for His answer and note down what you hear.

When God asks us to step into a new season, He never sends us there alone. He will be what we need Him to be in that season.

So, ask the Father to share with you what part of His character He wants to highlight in this season (it could be mercy, faithfulness, kindness, grace, goodness etc) and jot it down here.

. . . .

. . . .

. . . .

. . . .

Regularly asking these questions, will help us stay focused and on track with God's plans for our lives.

Spend some time listening to and reading His answers. Pray over the responsibilities currently in your hands. Declare the favour and peace of God over all you do. Ask to be stretched and for your capacity to grow, allowing more of God's purpose to be worked through you. Thank Him for another day.

'For we are God's handiwork, created in Christ Jesus to do good works, which God prepared in advance for us to do.' (Eph. 2:10)

Monday

Sometimes paradise comes with a few quirks.

'Therefore, since we are surrounded by such a great cloud of witnesses, let us throw off everything that hinders and the sin that so easily entangles. And let us run with perseverance the race marked out for us' (Heb. 12:1)

I've recently moved to a new flat, which I absolutely love. The location is perfect, the size is amazing for London, the colour scheme is beautiful and did I mention the location is perfect?

But there is this one thing about the lady in the flat above me. Well, two actually.

When she takes a shower it literally sounds like Niagara Falls in my bedroom. And she regularly arrives home to shower – at nearly midnight.

The second incessant, and ever so slightly annoying issue, has to do with exercise.

To a high impact fitness DVD.

Early in the morning.

You would think elephants were practising salsa dancing above my head.

And that isn't a comment on her size – I've seen her, and she is tiny. How on earth she makes the ceiling shake is beyond me.

But she does – and often just as I'm getting into a prayerful place in my devotions… 'Yes Lord, I love You Lord, Father God. You are amazing, Your Presence is…' BANG. BANG. BANG -de- BANG.

Sigh…

Have you ever had to fight for focus?

If we are to achieve anything of significance in life, battling the clamour of outside annoyances must be overcome. These may take the shape of a boss you find difficult, a child testing the boundaries, an unexpected bill, a husband forgetting to remove the rubbish *again*…

These annoyances will not go away.

But they are the very tools the enemy will use to threaten your peace – and ultimately your atmosphere.

I could blame my neighbour's exercising on ruining my time with God. Or I can turn up the worship music a bit louder and pray for an opportunity to share Christ with her.

'Set your minds on things that are above, not on things that are on earth.' (Col. 3:2, ESV)

Nobody else chooses my focus – only I do that. I choose where to look, what to think, who to listen to and how to respond. Perhaps today you are focusing on the wrong person? Is it possible the one you label 'enemy' is actually the one God labels 'test'? Or the frustration that is stealing your peace, is the tool that will strengthen your character?

Even if there *are* salsa dancing elephants above you...

Spend a few minutes thinking about your focus, and where it goes. What is the first thing you think of in the morning? The last at night? Where does your conversation tend to lean and with whom do you spend most of your time sharing your deepest thoughts? Does God factor into any of those scenerios? Focus is intentional, so this week be very intentional – give yourself time to think, ponder, and get honest. Have paper next to you, so when outside thoughts enter your quiet time, you can write them down and attend to them later.

Tuesday

Where I look reveals what I see.

> 'The word of the LORD came to me:
> "What do you see, Jeremiah?"
> "I see the branch of an almond tree," I replied.' (Jer. 1:11)

Jeremiah looked and saw what the Lord had revealed to him – an almond tree. He didn't see it in the natural, but as a vision in the spiritual. God was testing his ability to discern, knowing that he had a prophetic future speaking to the nations (Jer. 1:5).

If I were to ask you what you saw in your life right now, what would you answer? This isn't a trick question. Before you read any further, write down what you are seeing at the moment...

....

....

....

....

Is it positive or negative? Good or challenging?

....

....

....

....

Most likely it is a mix of both. Because both are needed for fruitfulness to occur. A life filled with only pleasure leads to laziness, and a life filled with only challenges leads to despair. It is the mix of both that creates the tapestry we present for the world to see. But as in all tapestries, we can see the front or the back – the beautiful picture or the twisted knots.

Spend some time right now praying over what you have seen. Not dwelling on either the negatives or positives, but praying blessing over *all* the Lord has currently allowed to enter your realm of personal oversight and accountability.

F ollowing Jeremiah's response to seeing the almond tree, the Lord answers: 'You have seen correctly, for I am watching to see that my word is fulfilled.' (Jer. 1:12)

The almond tree is the first tree to blossom – symbolising a waking up of sorts. The word 'watching' also means to be wakeful, showing that God is watching over His Word to make sure it is fulfilled.

Which do you see first – the hope or despair? The potential or the problems?

As God watches His Word to see it satisfied, we must watch and *expect* to see our potential unleashed. It will not happen by accident, nor by default. It happens as we partner with God – us doing our part and Him doing His part – just as with Jeremiah.

Read the following declaration a few times. Let it soak into your heart and let it awaken you to your purpose. I believe God is watching over His Word to perform it, and I believe He is watching over these words to outwork them. Remember, He loves you and has your best interest at heart!

I declare a waking up is happening in your world right now. A waking up to potential, to partnership, to purpose. I declare you are moving into a season of fruitfulness and favour. I declare you have eyes to see all the blessings of heaven waiting for you, a heart to receive, and a hand to respond. Your best days are ahead of you and as you fix your eyes on Jesus, He is making a way in the wilderness and a stream in the wasteland. See your potential. See the hope. See the future. And prepare yourself, ready to respond with a resounding YES to all He is asking of you. The future is bright, the boundaries are being extended, and what is before you is greater than what lies behind you!

Thursday

Focus changes everything – just ask a blind man.

In Mark 8:22–26 we see Jesus healing a blind man – in stages. Jesus spits on the man's eyes (yes, you read that right), covers them with His hands and then asks him what he sees.

The man replies: 'I see people; they look like trees walking around' (v24).

Now, clearly he wasn't referring to the Israelites in that day being the size of tree trunks; he meant his sight was blurred.

How easily that can happen.

We start down a path of excitedly serving the Lord, wanting to give our all and follow Him. We get a vision of how we can serve and where we can help, dreaming of fulfilling our mission. Then life happens.

And disappointment rudely walks in, without even knocking, taking a seat at the table of our contentment, spilling water all over our dreams.

Someone today needs to try again.

Stop blaming the past, your parents, the husband, life – or God.

Are there any figures of blame that come to your mind now? Write them down.

....

....

....

You can choose how you will respond. It's time to clean up the mess, reset the table, add some flowers and rediscover who God has made you to be.

Take some time to pray over that picture, asking God to put it into focus. Journal your thoughts and hear what the Holy Spirit wants to say to you...

....

....

....

Friday

Any person of sport knows that without focus, a team will probably lose.

And yet, according to some studies, we have a limited period of focused time before our alertness begins to wane. Without a break, we become lethargic and less productive.

In other words, *change is beneficial.*

This is especially true in the spiritual seasons of our lives. God allows events which may challenge us, yet He is ever present in those events to further champion us. If we believe God is working all things together for good (Rom. 8:28) then we can trust Him in every season.

If there has been a 'change of season' for you recently, see it as an opportunity to renew your focus. Seek the Lord for what He is doing and ask Him how you can partner with Him in it.

WEEK 5: ELEPHANT IN THE ROOM

Father, thank You that You are *for* me, not against me. Thank You for Your kindness and grace. Thank You that I am on Your mind, at this exact moment. And thank You that Your heart beats with love for me and for my future. I want to fully live out my destiny, seeing dreams unfold and miracles spring forth. To do this, I must trust You. So I declare now that I believe in You, I receive Your goodness and I live to glorify Your name. Help me live this season fully – not holding back out of fear or disappointment – looking for opportunities to spread the joy of a life lived with You and for You. It's a pleasure. And a privilege. Amen.

Write here your own thoughts, or what you sense God may be saying to you.

....

....

....

....

Monday

I was given
nine weeks.

'His lord said to him, "Well *done*, good and
faithful servant; you were faithful over a few
things, I will make you ruler over many things.
Enter into the joy of your lord."'
(Matt. 25:21, NKJV)

The phone call came one Tuesday morning, completely out of the blue. I was innocently working at my desk when an unknown number showed on my phone. Upon answering it, a man from the Alzheimer's Society explained that a runner had dropped out of the London Marathon and did I want to take his place?

Marathon? Take his place? Altogether now, let's say...
wrong number.

He said it again – this time with slightly more urgency to his voice, explaining that I only had a few hours to make the decision, otherwise they would find someone else. Oh, and in addition I was required to raise £2000 in those nine weeks.

I put down the phone and tried to pray. But the most I could do was squeak out an 'Oh Jesus…' whilst pacing around my lounge.

Nine weeks to morph running an average of five miles into a total of 26.2 miles. Nine weeks to raise £2000. And during week five, I would be moving 200 miles up north to a new city/new church/new job.

No biggie.

This should have been a no brainer – emphasis on the word 'NO'!

But something inside me couldn't let it go.

I had set a goal earlier in the year of running a marathon, but when I didn't make the ballot I thought the chance had gone. Now it suddenly reappeared. The opportunity didn't look like I thought it would, wasn't in the timing I wanted and it came with a myriad of additional challenges – but at its core, *it was what I had asked for.*

Life often gives what we ask for, but rarely does it look like we expect.

In fact, we may receive what we ask for, only to wonder why we asked! We see the answer and wish we had posed a different question.

What I discovered from running the marathon (in 4:53:36 I might add!), was that *the investment inside overcame the obstacles outside.*

Nine weeks was enough training, because I had over twenty years of three miles here, five miles there…

And it's the same with you.

Where have you invested and are expecting a harvest? It could be financially, emotionally, educationally, with children or grandchildren, time, spiritually... investment is endless. Write out some investments you are still believing in for a harvest, then pray over the investment again, asking God's blessing and return.

....

....

....

....

Remember *every* prayer time, Bible reading, worship song and wise choice will reap benefits beyond the ability you envision or even think you can carry.

Intentionally invest.

Tuesday

Don't look for your purpose, experience it.

Too many people falsely believe their purpose is 'out there' somewhere, and if they try hard enough it will either knock on their door or be found underfoot one serendipitous day. They spend their lives in search of the elusive arrival of their purpose in life, not realising their accomplishments are found throughout the journey, and not at the finish line.

Purpose is found in our everyday living – the sometimes boring, other times exciting, day-to-day life that we live. Out of the ordinary comes our extraordinary moments, woven into the fabric of our lives, word by word and season by season.

Once we embrace this concept, we free ourselves from the tyranny of fear, which says we will ultimately miss what we continually seek.

What an important statement, let me reiterate it: *being thankful for what is in front of us is the first step toward disempowering the fear of 'missing it'.*

Yet, in order to embrace and experience fullness of purpose, we must regularly conquer one reappearing mountain we all prefer to detour: RISK.

Without risk we remain tied to a world of safety, secure in the home of the known and captivated by the village of the familiar.

There is no fulfilled purpose without risk. Because purpose is not something we control, it is something we discover.

What are some of the biggest risks you have taken in life?

....

....

What have the positive outcomes been? The negative?

....

....

Out of 1–10 (10 being 'completely willing'), how willing at this moment are you to take a risk for the possibility of receiving what you are hoping for?

....

....

....

Father God, risk has at times been a friend and other times an enemy. But I do not want fear to control my level of risk; I want risk to quiet the strength of my fear. Please help me risk within limits and only as I'm led by Your Spirit. Give me peace where You want me to move forward, caution where You want me to stop and wisdom to know the difference. Thank You that You are for me, not against me. And thank You that You only desire my best. Be glorified in me and through me today – and every day. Amen.

Wednesday

Yesterday we talked about risk, today let's look at reward. In Judges 6, Gideon was in a winepress, depressed, defeated and despondent over the state of affairs in his life and the lives of his people. He had dreamed of freedom over the years, only to see it endlessly elude him through repeated defeat and disappointment at the hand of the Midianites.

So God shows up one day and reminds him of his investment.

'When the angel of the LORD appeared to Gideon, he said, "The LORD is with you, mighty warrior."' (Judg. 6:12)

God would not have spoken what was untrue. Therefore, over the years an investment had been made by Gideon to be trained as a warrior and surrendered as a worshipper. Inside, Gideon had all he needed to perform one of the greatest victories ever accomplished. Yet to Gideon, his years of investment looked to culminate in a winepress and with a whimper.

'"Pardon me, my lord," Gideon replied, "but if the LORD is with us, why has all this happened to us? Where are all his wonders that our ancestors told us about… how can I save Israel? My clan is the weakest in Manasseh, and I am the least in my family."' (Judg. 6:13,15)

When we see ourselves apart from the miraculous power of God, all will look impossible and we will never believe we are up for the task.

Once Gideon took a risk and trusted God, then his rewards came fast and furious.

Judges 6:25–29 shows us that fear no longer ruled Gideon. In Judges 6:34–35 we see God's favour over Gideon's life as 32,000 men chose to follow his leadership, and in Judges 8:10 Gideon touched the miraculous when his 300 men defeated 120,000 enemy soldiers.

Boldness, favour and the miraculous – none of these rewards would have happened if Gideon hadn't taken a God-fuelled risk.

What is a dream of yours that is yet unfulfilled?

....

....

....

What are the risks and rewards around pursuing this dream?

....

....

....

Thursday

I ntentionally invest.

Let's revisit that phrase from Monday's reading today.

According to the *Oxford English Dictionary*, the word 'intentional' means 'done on purpose; deliberate' and 'invest' means 'devote (one's time, effort, or energy) to a particular undertaking with the expectation of a worthwhile result'.

So to intentionally invest would mean: *deliberately devoting time, energy and effort to a particular task, expecting a worthwhile result.*

Where do you intentionally invest? And is it done expecting a *worthwhile result*?

Define 'worthwhile result' – what does that look like for you?

Most of us have areas in our lives where we intentionally invest – relationships, finances, health to name a few. But do we always expect a worthwhile result from our investment? Sometimes it is done more out of duty and discipline, with a focus on action rather than outcome.

Jesus invested in the twelve disciples, more specifically three (Peter, James, John), believing that His investment would impact the nations.

Even at the end of His life, the investment looked to have failed – they all ran away from Him at His time of greatest need. Peter was the worst culprit, actually denying He even knew Jesus. Yet after the resurrection, one of the first acts of mercy Jesus performed was to reinstate Peter's position and purpose to lead (John 21).

Intentionality does that. It looks for opportunities until the last moment, even at times when the opportunity looks missed. It does not surrender to the negative, but keeps its eyes on the expected end result.

Is there anything, or anyone, distracting you today from investing in your future? What about investing in the future of another?

. . . .

. . . .

. . . .

Be intentional. Not only for your own miracle, but for the miracle of another.

Friday

Gideon trusted God, which tells me there was an investment of faith built in his life, seeing the miraculous as a result. And then he invested into the lives of his men, giving them an opportunity to be part of something bigger than they'd ever dreamed – defeating the enemy's army by being one of only 300 people to touch this miracle. They saw risk as worth the reward. And it was.

Read the story of Gideon again (Judg. 6–8) and think about your own life as you read it. In which areas are you 'hiding in a winepress' and in which areas are you being asked by God to take a risk? Note any thoughts that come to you here.

As you think through this story, and this week's devotionals, journal any further thoughts and discoveries here. Let the Holy Spirit reveal the heart of God to you and for you in this season.

By the way... four weeks ago I promised to remind you of what you wrote in week two (on page 31) – how are you getting on with the changes you set in place on your calendar? If you've forgotten, now is a good time to review them and renew your commitment to change!

. . . .

. . . .

. . . .

Notes

Part 3

Heart

WHY YOU ARE

'Delight yourself in the LORD; And He will give you the desires of your heart. Commit your way to the LORD, Trust also in Him, and He will do it.' (Psa. 37:4–5, NASB)

Monday

Are you cheeky?

Y ou know the type. Asking for extras, looking for favours, hoping for a handout.

Lately I've heard the term 'cheeky beggar' bounced around like a volleyball at the beach. Upon first hearing it I was put off, thinking a good Christian should not be seen as trying to get something for nothing. This is the type of thing that gives Christians a bad reputation – we are meant to be generous, not stingy.

But then I observed cheekiness in action.

Asking for property at a ridiculous price, knowing the money saved will further the kingdom; believing for a job well outside your qualifications, knowing the potential for kingdom influence will be greater; asking for extra toppings on your ice cream… just because (one can't super-spiritualise *everything!*).

And suddenly my vision changed.

I wasn't only begging for me, I was asking for Him.

This wasn't to increase my own gains, it was to make His name famous.

So, I am learning that there *are* times to ask for, and expect, a blessing, because we already know from Scripture that God wants to bless us (see Eph. 1:3; Jer. 29:11; Psa. 1:1–6; Phil. 4:19).

And there *are* moments to risk embarrassment, because we see a purpose beyond ourselves in our asking, knowing God is already watching out for our interests.

Christianity has somehow turned boldness into thinking more highly of yourself than you ought. Who are we to ask for a favour? To expect a discount? To seek a bargain? We are meant to be quiet, submissive and wait until the door opens for us.

That's simply not true. At least, not all of the time.

There are times to keep knocking on that door, asking God

for advancement, and seeking windows of opportunity, until immovable situations experience serendipitous outcomes.

Can you think of a time when you've experienced this in your life? A time you saw change as a result of your boldness?

....

....

....

....

To really see cheeky in action, look at the One we adore: Jesus took a boy's only meal away from him with no explanation; He watched a widow give all she had left to an offering and said nothing to her; He asked men to give up their livelihood and serve, no questions asked.

Now *that* is cheeky…

Take a few minutes to think about how you would define 'cheeky'. Write out what it means to you, in a positive way – what that looks like. Would you consider yourself to be a cheeky person? Do you struggle asking for favours, and if so why? Ask the Lord to increase your boldness and confidence!

....

....

....

....

Tuesday

Bold is beautiful.

When I was younger I couldn't look at a stranger without my face morphing into a bright red glow, one akin to Rudolph's nose as he pulled Santa's sleigh. To ask someone a question… you might have thought I was confronting members of the UN. My mind went blank, mouth dry and face numb. Petrified does not even begin to describe how I lived a good portion of my teenage and young adult years…

Yet what is my calling?

Speaking to crowds.

Does anyone else see the conflict in this little scenario?

Our fulfilled calling is inevitably found on the other side of our conquered weakness.

And once one weakness has been conquered, another will rise up to take its place. That is simply the nature of humanity, the price for living courageous lives and the beauty in surrendering all to follow Jesus.

Which weakness is the Lord dealing with in your life at the moment?

....

....

....

What has been placed in your life to allow that weakness to be brought front and centre?

....

....

....

Know that whatever you are facing, God already knows you can conquer. He has given you strength for all that you face and He has promised never to leave you, nor forsake you, in your journey (Heb. 13:5).

Take some time to read the following prayer and sit in His presence… Let Him release love on you…

Father, thank You for Your presence, which is with me right now. I invite You, Holy Spirit, to minister Your grace, peace and calm to my spirit. I ask that You help me feel and know Your presence in a tangible way. I declare 'peace be still' over my situation and my life. And Father, I thank You that You are greater than my greatest weakness and You are stronger than my strongest fear. I choose You. I choose truth. And I choose joy. I love You. Amen.

Wednesday

I am going to say it again: Bold is beautiful.

In Judges 4 we see Deborah as a prophet, wife, judge and leader. She was well respected and knew her mind, but more so knew the voice of God. She was unafraid of conflict and led with precision – decisive and direct.

Today we would see her in a corporate boardroom or organising a fundraiser. Others would be following and she wouldn't hesitate to give directions, to women *and* men.

As women, we must not fear leading.

Leading is not masculine or feminine, it is kingdom. God created us to be leaders – influencers – of our world, *all* of us.

And to lead will take courage, boldness, a quiet spirit and a calm mind. All of which you have in the fruit of the Spirit (Gal. 5:22–23).

Do you hesitate to lead, and if so why?

....

....

....

Remember, you can lead in many different ways (eg large groups, small groups, individual mentoring, organising by team, directing by example etc). Perhaps one of these stands out to you today?

· ·

· ·

· ·

If you have a tendency to shy away from leading, ask the Lord for boldness. Ask Him to bring out the leadership gifting inside of you. And realise that to do so will mean confronting some of your greatest fears at the moment. BUT YOU CAN DO IT! You really can. With God's help – *all* things truly are possible. Trust Him.

I sense some women reading this know you are meant to step into leadership, yet you have been afraid. Write below where you feel God is leading you, and then write the next step toward involvement in that area. Just write one step – then go do it!

· ·

· ·

· ·

· ·

Thursday

For some of us, fearing leadership isn't the issue, controlling pride is.

We believe we are born to lead and we have no hesitation in letting other people know that our opinion is not only a good one, it's the right one!

If that's you (and even if it's not!) then let's take a few minutes today exploring not thinking of yourself 'more highly than you ought' (Rom. 12:3).

Romans 12 starts by saying we should offer our bodies as 'living sacrifices', which is an act of worship.

According to the *Oxford English Dictionary*, sacrifice by definition means to 'give up (something valued) for the sake of other considerations'.

Though our lives are valued, and we are to value them, there is a higher purpose for our breathing and that is the will and call of God for our lives. Not calling the shots, so to speak, is one of the most difficult tests we must face as Christians. It involves trusting that God knows best, even if it seems polar opposite to our desires.

Which areas of your life do you find difficult to
trust God with?

....

....

....

Part of being a 'living sacrifice' is not conforming to
the pattern of this world. Be honest, does the pull of
the world (fashion, finances, appearance, property etc)
have a hold on your heart?

....

....

....

When it comes to the subject of pride, there's a pitfall to look out
for. That is, there's a fine balance between humility and the trap
of self-deprecation, denial or martyrdom. Living the Christian
life is the best life there is, and celebrating ourselves should be
a daily joy!

So we must simply keep celebration in line with sacrifice –
knowing that as we embrace both, we walk in the perfect balance
of self-appreciation and God-adoration.

Friday

L et's go back to Monday's devotional and the theme for this
week: Cheeky Beggar.

Do you find it easy to ask for what you (really) want?

. . . .

. . . .

. . . .

If yes, celebrate and thank the Lord for breakthrough in this area.
Then… ask Him to expand your faith and give you even GREATER
requests to believe for!

If no, admit it… and ask the Lord for a 'spirit of cheekiness'!

Further on in Romans 12:3, it refers to 'the measure of faith' (ESV)
God has given you. This alludes again to not thinking of yourself
more highly than you ought. But I want to point out – we have *all*
been given a measure of faith.

Don't worry about how big or small that measure is, worry about
using all of it and leaving none behind. Remember the banana
bread I tried to bake in week three? The bread didn't rise and
people weren't fed, all because I didn't use the full measurement
of what was required.

We have already been given the full amount of faith we need to do what God is asking us to do.

Our job is to:

1. believe it, and

2. act on it.

And to do this in confidence, not pride and for His glory, not our own.

If we do not do this, people's lives will not be impacted (fed) and we will not fulfil all that God created us for.

Spend some time pondering Romans12:1–8, and write down your thoughts here.

....

....

....

Monday

Mirrors – it's a love/hate relationship.

'But he said to me, "My grace is sufficient for you, for my power is made perfect in weakness." Therefore I will boast all the more gladly about my weaknesses, so that Christ's power may rest on me.' (2 Cor. 12:9)

Y eah, you feel it too?

My issue isn't with all mirrors though, nope – only the ones you find in hotel rooms on the side of the bathroom wall.

You know the one – you turn to look at it and suddenly your face has morphed into a mirage of pores and wrinkles – with big eyeballs staring out from the middle – because this lovely contraption is meant to not just show your face, but show *every detail* of your face!

And for the record may I just say, I don't think mirrors should be made to get us that close to our faces. Some things simply are not meant to be magnified!

Now, I realise these mirrors are normally for shaving. Which, to be fair, I would want if I was putting a sharp razor near my neck and moving it vertically at a rapid pace.

But for the average woman… we'd rather not look at our faces with a magnifying glass, thank you.

I often stay in a hotel room when I'm travelling for work. And so frequently I find myself brushing my teeth, then suddenly getting a fright when I look to my right – and see myself (my pores) staring back at me from the wall.

Wrinkles I hadn't noticed, freckles (these couldn't possibly be age spots) stepping into the limelight, stray chin hair (*what is THAT all about, God?!*) popping out to wave and say 'hello' – they're all there.

Close up.

All our lives carry disparity from the distance to the detail, with distance creating illusions only detail will reveal.

If we never allow anyone to see the detail, the disparity grows and the illusion becomes our reality.

If we allow the wrong person to see it, their fixation with our detail allows no freedom for tangible change.

Enter – GRACE.

God sees the detail, is under no illusions, and loves us anyway.

So what *exactly* does God see when He looks at us close up?

Generosity or greed? Love or anger? Peace or unrest?

If we want a mirror such as this, how often should we give it to others walking the path alongside us?

What does grace mean to you? Ponder, or write out, your own definition and then spend time thanking God for His grace toward you today.

....

....

....

....

Tuesday

We tend to judge our mundane by others' highlights.

Instagram has become a social media phenomenon. You post pictures of everything from holidays, to children, to your cup of coffee and random strangers. Anything in sight is up for grabs and has the potential to be 'filtered' into looking bright and beautiful, when in reality it was dull and grey.

William Blake once declared: *'I will not reason and compare, my business is to create.'* Similarly Mark Twain upheld that *'Comparison is the death of joy'.*

Actions fuelled by comparison lack creativity and uniqueness, eventually breeding similarity.

We cannot freely move forward into our purpose if we continually compare ourselves with others. And yet, asking a woman to stop comparing is like asking a dog to stop sniffing! The opportunities are too plentiful and the fear of missing something too great!

Before we go any further, we must be honest with ourselves: how often do you compare yourself to others? Is it only in certain areas (appearance, work, parenting) or do you find yourself in the comparison trap in all areas?

'Make a careful exploration of who you are and the work you have been given, and then sink yourself into that. Don't be impressed with yourself. Don't compare yourself with others. Each of you must take responsibility for doing the creative best you can with your own life.' (Gal. 6:4–5, *The Message*)

Can you think of anyone you compare yourself to? Why is that? What unique parts of yourself can you hear God telling you to focus on? Journal your thoughts here:

....

....

....

....

....

Wednesday

In John 21 we see a conversation between Peter and Jesus – the first since Peter's denial of Jesus at His arrest and Jesus' subsequent death and resurrection. Jesus and Peter are now sitting around a campfire eating cod, when Jesus asks Peter if he loves Him.

Peter replies, 'Yes, Lord... you know that I love you.' (John 21:15)

The question is repeated twice, with the same answer, and then Jesus speaks a bit about Peter's future and finally declares, 'Follow me!' (v19).

As opposed to saying thank You and joyfully accepting the invitation to once again serve and spend time with his Saviour and Friend, Peter instead asks what is going to happen to John. Peter and John don't see eye to eye on all things, their personalities are polar opposites, and here we see Peter wondering if after the resurrection his company will *still* involve John.

In other words – is he coming too, Jesus?!

Jesus basically rebukes Peter and says that it's none of his business; his only concern was to follow.

Comparing our lives with others puts our energy and attention in the wrong place.

We cannot move forward if we continually take our eyes off Jesus and look at others.

Where in your life has Jesus said 'Follow me', and have you done this wholeheartedly? Or is there a part of you looking around to see who else is coming with you?

. . . .

. . . .

. . . .

What part of following Jesus has been the most difficult for you?

. . . .

. . . .

. . . .

Thursday

God sees the detail, is under no illusions, and loves us anyway.

How does re-reading this line from Monday's devotional make you feel? Do you believe it?

Only in knowing and receiving His love are we set free to fully know and love others. The more I receive His love, the freer I offer my love.

Grace is complex, beautiful, misunderstood, simple, tangible and hard to describe… As something we don't deserve, we may find it difficult to receive and even more challenging to give. Yet grace makes an appearance when we are at our lowest (2 Cor. 12:9). It is the door to salvation (Eph. 2:5) and the throne from which mercy flows (Heb. 4:16).

'Amazing grace, how sweet the sound that saved a wretch like me. I once was lost, but now am found, was blind but now I see.' Words penned by a former slave trader – a man who brutalised the lives of others, yet a man who learned that his past was no indication of his future.

Your past does not define you. And failure is an event, not an identity.

Again – *failure is an event, not an identity.*

Look up the scriptures from today in your Bible – read them slowly and digest their truths.

Write here what grace means to you… Do you sense God's acceptance, even in your failures?

. . . .

. . . .

. . . .

. . . .

Father, thank You for Your love and especially for Your grace. Grace that forgives and sets free. Grace that covers our sin and unveils Your love. I receive this grace. In all areas of my life right now, I receive Your grace. Amen.

Take some time simply to sit in His presence and receive this grace over your life…

Friday

'Heal the sick, raise the dead, cleanse those who have leprosy, drive out demons. *Freely you have received; freely give'* (Matt. 10:8, emphasis mine).

As we receive grace, we are called to give grace.

When we see our imperfections are accepted by a loving God, and when we stop striving for perfection as the pinnacle of our success, we can begin championing someone other than ourselves.

And as we celebrate others' successes and help others fulfil their dreams, God sees that ours are also fulfilled. But if we fixate on the errors of others, using it to elevate our own status, then we refuse to grow the character needed for our destiny.

True destiny unfolds only as much as it benefits others and glorifies God.

Are you able to champion others above yourself?

How do you put others first – not in a self-deprecating, but in a life-giving way?

. . . .

. . . .

. . . .

Is there anyone you struggle to celebrate? Why?

. . . .

. . . .

. . . .

Ask the Lord for the grace, and the opportunity, to celebrate this person in the future… Be willing to give, as you have received – freely.

Monday

I choose the quiet coach in order to have quiet.

'I can do all this through him who gives me strength.' (Phil. 4:13)

Call me pedantic – and yes, in this area I am a bit (a lot) – but if a train coach is labelled 'quiet', and it is clearly marked on *every* window that there should be 'no unnecessary noise', then that is what I expect.

Every week I get the early train up north for work and every week I sit in the quiet carriage, hoping for the best. Today was no different. Except, due to the London Underground being delayed, my stress level was elevated and I thought I would be late.

My biggest concern wasn't actually missing the train, it was missing my Starbucks latte, which always accompanies me on the train.

Thankfully, we both made it.

But once seated and whilst still waiting to depart, a group of lovely people boarded. Talking loudly. Laughing (how dare they). Enjoying themselves (it's 7:24am, people).

Basically – they annoyed me.

But something annoyed me even more than they did.

After thirty minutes, the train manager came to check tickets. As they were talking loudly at the time, I was certain he would say something. I watched (told you I was pedantic) from the other end of the train – nothing.

How could he NOT say something to them? This is the *quiet carriage* and they were *not* being quiet.

So when he got to me I said something. Very quietly (wouldn't want them to know it was me), I mentioned the people up front making noise and would he please kindly remind them this is the quiet carriage.

He looked terrified.

Seriously, buddy – it's not that difficult. And by the way, *it's your job*.

I repeated the question. He quite clearly was uncertain what to do and was not enamoured with confrontation.

He finally mumbled something and, turning, he *slowly* walked toward them. Suddenly he pretended to be looking for something else, then turned around, quickly walking down the aisle past me (no eye contact), and out of the carriage.

He caved.

Though he had the authority, he did not have the courage.

Courage is a necessary ingredient to living a life of influence. Without it we will surrender to the loudest voice, but with it we silence the strongest enemy.

As we board the quiet coach together and begin to reflect on this week's devotionals, think about if there was ever a time you failed to follow through, due to fear? God was leading you in a particular direction, but you couldn't find the courage to obey? There's no shame or guilt in that, we are human. At the beginning of this week, think about your level of courage, about what things make you shy away from moving forward, and about God's grace to confront those areas with boldness and a new conviction. Then take time to write down how courageous you feel you are at this stage in your life, and where you want to be in the future.

....

....

....

....

111

'Fear not' is one of the most quoted phrases in the Bible. Although I am yet to actually count for myself, I've heard preachers say it is in there 365 times – one mention for every day of the year!

Fear is something that grips most of us on a regular basis. From minor fears of attending a meeting or making small talk, to larger fears of raising our children or battling an illness.

Life takes courage.

Without courage we cannot fulfil our purpose.

When Joshua was given the assignment to lead the Israelites to the promised land, some of his first words of encouragement from the Lord were, 'Be strong and courageous' (Josh. 1:6).

What would it take for you to walk in more courage? What is holding you back?

....

....

....

Anything that weighs us down is not of God – what fears are weighing heavy on your heart today?

....

....

....

Google (or look in your concordance for) verses that have the phrase 'fear not' in them. Meditate on their truths – write them out if it's helpful – and choose one to memorise, so it's at the ready when you need it.

....

....

....

Thank You, Lord, that You do not give a spirit of fear. But You give power, love and a sound mind to have a good, hard look at life – and then the strength to fully dive in, knowing that You will never leave me nor forsake me. Give me more courage, Lord! Help me throw aside anything hindering me from fully running this race, and thank You for giving me all that I need, to do ALL that You've created me to do! Amen.

Wednesday

T he moment when quiet needed to be championed,
he chose silence. This refers back to Monday's devotional and
the train manager, who could not manage.
Have you ever bailed out when you should have stepped in? Does
your voice weaken at the moments it should speak?

God needs His girls vocal, strong, confident and courageous. We
were designed and created to be this way! I'm not talking about a
personality that is unsubmissive, rude, bolshie or prideful, but I am
encouraging a beautiful, velvet steel type of strength. One who
knows who she is, and who is unafraid to confidently move in the
direction of her destiny.

Courage will not be created without fear.

Therefore, we must embrace fear as the springboard to greater
courage, open doors and timely promotion.

In other words, fear at the beginning shows us there is promotion
at the end. *Instead of focusing on the fear, believe for the promotion.*
This will help you push through your fear…

What fear is in the way of your promotion at the moment? (Promotion does not only signify a job – it could be a new relationship, a leadership position, greater finances, a dream fulfilled etc.)

....

....

....

Refer back to the 'fear not' scriptures you looked up yesterday – what would God say to you about this obstacle, using those scriptures as your backdrop?

....

....

....

Thursday

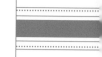

The courageous… move.

One of the scariest things I've ever needed to do was force myself to jump.

Out of an airplane. 15,000 feet in the air.

My mind screamed at me, the logic taunted me, and the wind dared me to defy it.

But once I jumped – pure, unadulterated… FREEDOM.

Making a move sets in motion more than our physical body. It allows God to direct, nature to affect, and hope to project what could be in place of what is. Motion creates new opportunities and movement takes us places we never would have seen otherwise.

The hardest move we have to make is not necessarily the first step – it is the step directly in front of us.

For Peter it was stepping out of the boat, for Stephen it was stepping up to speak truth, for Esther it was stepping into the king's court and for Jesus it was stepping up to the cross.

Each step was excruciatingly difficult, with varied consequences, but life-changing results.

Imagine if none of them had taken the steps they did.
We wouldn't be challenged by a human successfully having walked on water, Saul wouldn't have been forever impacted from seeing Stephen die with joy, the Jewish people could have potentially been annihilated and salvation would not be ours today.

Your step may not have the impact that theirs did, but it *will* have an impact. Not the least on your courage, once you have stepped – experienced – and overcome.

I implore you not to procrastinate on what the Holy Spirit is prompting. To do so may not only affect your future, but the future of many others.

Dare to dream.

What would the best-case scenario of that dream look like? Be honest and describe it here.

Friday

Have you ever woken from an exciting dream, only to realise it was fantasy, and the life you were living in that dream existed outside reality?

There was probably a letdown, a sorrow, or maybe it created an excitement for what could have been…

Dreams can simultaneously be empowering and also intimidating. This devotional isn't the place to explore why we dream, and the interpretations behind those dreams. But it is a place to remember that dreams exist, and at the most basic they are used to work out what has been worked *in* to our lives.

Dreams are not only meant for the night time. They are to be lived in the daylight.

Dream again.

That's a statement for someone. You need to dream again. Chance again. Hope again. And try again. Enough is enough and the season of mourning is over! It's time to dance, to rejoice, to love, to LIVE.

Dreams are not only about ourselves, they must reach a world beyond our personal borders.

Remind yourself of the dream you wrote about
yesterday, who will it impact for good?

· ·

· ·

· ·

Notes

Part 4

Feet

WHERE YOU ARE

'So don't sit around on your hands! No more dragging your feet! Clear the path for long-distance runners so no one will trip and fall, so no one will step in a hole and sprain an ankle. Help each other out. And run for it!' (Heb. 12:12–13, *The Message*)

Monday

You dropped this.

Three seemingly kind words meant to assist… yet in this particular instance, meant anything but assistance.

It was the centre of London, at midnight and I was lost.

After a great night spending four hours chatting to a friend, I began walking toward the tube station. I wasn't nervous as I'd done this many times late at night, and there were still people milling about.

But directions and I are not friends.

In fact, if I ever tell you to turn right – go left immediately.

So within five minutes I was lost, and found myself in a quiet and slightly rougher street in London.

'No worries,' I thought, just follow the blue dot on your Google Maps and you will be fine.

The blue dot and I are not friends.

The situation became worse and soon I was completely turned around, when suddenly I tripped on the pavement. That's when I heard those words.

A car slowed down in the road. Coming to a stop, the man lowered his window and said: 'You dropped this.' Being tired, I was confused and looked back at the pavement, wondering what I had dropped. I couldn't see clearly what was in his hands, and I took one step closer.

He repeated it – 'You dropped this', slightly more emphatically.

I began approaching the car to investigate, when suddenly inside me alarm bells went off.

Dark windows. Midnight. London. He's concealing what is in his hand.

I stepped away and said, 'No thank you, I'm fine.' A dark cloud went over his face and he spun his car away.

I hailed a taxi and within twenty seconds was safely on my way home.

Sometimes a helping hand becomes a divisive grip. The enemy masquerades as the kind assistant, when behind the charm is an impostor waiting for the take down.

Real assistance results in peace, is covered in grace and drives us forward.

What about you? Is your assistance offered with any ulterior motives?

. . . .

. . . .

. . . .

How are you at promoting others beyond yourself?
Who are you mentoring to the next level?

. . . .

. . . .

. . . .

Ask God at the beginning of this week to reveal anyone
you are meant to be assisting, whilst also showing you
anyone who is draining you more than is necessary and
right for you at this time.

Tuesday

'Never be afraid to trust an unknown future to a known God.' – Corrie ten Boom

Trust is an emotive word.

I mean, who hasn't lost the trust of a girlfriend by age seven in school? She promises she is your best friend, but then when your back is turned she becomes friends with… *her*!

Watching the fickleness of children can be somewhat humorous, but seeing the fierceness of adults can be deeply troubling. Again – who hasn't experienced the betrayal of one you thought was a confidant and friend, or even a spouse?

By adulthood each one of us has experienced the pain of rejection and, maybe, the dagger of deception. Having a relationship tested often causes us to retreat into the security of self, protecting ourselves from the potential of pain through trusting again. And every layer of casing around our hearts creates barriers not only here on earth, but potentially in our relationship with God.

If those walls are not broken down, we will miss the opportunity to love deeply… and to be loved deeply. To be influenced, *and to influence.*

Letting past hurt control present hope is damaging.

It is impossible to move forward into all God has for us if we hold on to past hurts. Your future is huge; don't let the past become the hurdle which trips you up from reaching the finish line.

Ask the Holy Spirit to reveal if there is any hurt controlling you, which needs to be dropped and left in the palm of God's grace?

. . . .

. . . .

. . . .

Father, I want to trust You, deeper than I already do. You are my Father as well as my Friend. Sometimes I only see authority and I miss Your authenticity. Your authentic love, grace, strength, goodness... all of which are available to me right now. I receive that authenticity with no hesitation and I let go of any preconceived ideas that You cannot be trusted. Regardless of my past, You are good. Regardless of my present, You are good. Reaching into my future, You, are, GOOD. Amen.

Wednesday

'*Then Saul went to Jerusalem. He tried to join the group* of followers, but they were all afraid of him. They did not believe that he was really a follower of Jesus. *But Barnabas accepted Saul* and took him to the apostles. He told them how Saul had seen the Lord on the road and how the Lord had spoken to Saul. Then he told them how boldly Saul had spoken for the Lord in Damascus. And so Saul stayed with the followers and went all around Jerusalem speaking boldly for the Lord' (Acts 9:26–28, ERV, emphasis mine).

We all long to be accepted.

We all struggle to accept.

Barnabas was willing to gamble his reputation on one whose own reputation included a CV filled with murder and judgment. He befriended the despised and championed the fanatic.

Acceptance does that.

Understanding our own identity frees us to liberate others. Barnabas knew his strength – encouragement. His name (which means 'Son of Encouragement') embodied his purpose, giving him parameters within which he sought opportunity to be used.

If Barnabas' name described him as 'encouragement' – what name would you give yourself at the moment?

. . . .

. . . .

. . . .

. . . .

What name do you aspire to be? Why?

. . . .

. . . .

. . . .

. . . .

Thursday

Real assistance results in peace, is covered in grace, and drives us forward.

You may recognise this from Monday's devotional. It challenges us to think about assistance and what that really looks like.

Have you ever had someone offer you a helping hand, which ultimately became additional work, as opposed to ease of assignment?

Often this comes in the form of a little one, wanting to help mum or dad! Their little hearts are sincere, but their little hands are far from skilled, taking your patience to a whole new level.

Jesus was clearly patience personified as He worked with the likes of Peter and… well, Peter!

Peter had real issues with pride, impulsiveness, judgment, and … pride. In John 13:8, Peter tells Jesus not to wash his feet, in Matthew 16:22 he boldly rebukes the Lord (who does that?!) and in John 18:17,25,27 he actually denies even knowing the Lord… three times.

Peter. He was one of a kind, yet… exactly like all of us.

Which is why we can learn from the way Jesus handled Peter.

Throughout all of those wrong choices and bad attitudes, Jesus treated Peter as a beloved friend and potential world changer. He changed his name (Matt. 16:18), forgave him (John 21:15–19) and honoured him as one of His closest disciples (Matthew. 17:1–3). Grace doesn't look for perfection. It is perfection, personified in Christ.

Mentoring others involves us seeing potential in the broken and believing the best out of the worst. It can be influencing without words, simply through behaviour.

We must get beyond our own world, into the world of another. If we don't – we haven't truly lived. We have only existed.

What keeps you from intentionally mentoring another? (Fear, pride, insecurity, self-absorption, lack of confidence?)

Friday

If you have lived more than a few years, you have something to teach. A five-year-old 'mentors' a two-year-old – watch them play together. We have all learned *something* that can be used to bless and help another. That, in its most basic form, is mentoring.

And that, in its most basic form, is something we all can do.

In Exodus 17:9 Moses tells Joshua to secure an army and fight the Amalekites, as he stands above them with arms outstretched watching, praying and overseeing. It's the beginning of Joshua's training, which will see him forty years later conquering Canaan without the aid of Moses.

So how did Moses help Joshua go from helper to leader?

As we close this week we will look at part one of the story, with parts two and three in the following weeks.

Firstly – Moses gave Joshua an opportunity.

Moses asked him to step up into a position of leadership, but he watched over Joshua as he did so. This is prior to Joshua's time worshipping in the tent of meeting, his succeeding Moses after his death, his declaring the walls of Jericho to fall, or the defeat of Canaan. He was just a young guy called on to fight one battle.

Opportunity opened the way for advancement.

Who around you is looking for an opportunity to be challenged, to grow, to learn or be given responsibility? (Don't only look for the obvious – Jesus used unschooled fishermen to change the world.)

Whatever position you hold, always look for someone you can raise up to take your place and/or learn from what you do.

Ask the Holy Spirit to show you – either now or in the next few weeks – who you can help succeed, by coming alongside them with encouragement and opportunity. Pray for that person (or people) now – believing God will open a door for your relationship to grow.

Monday

I've always wondered what it would be like...

'Arise, shine, for your light has come, and the glory of the LORD rises upon you. See, darkness covers the earth and thick darkness is over the peoples, but the LORD rises upon you and his glory appears over you.' (Isa. 60:1–2)

I had heard of them, known their reputation and been intrigued by them for years.

Were they as good as people say? Did they really work? Could it truly be possible?

Then I moved to a new flat in London and discovered them for myself.

Blackout curtains.

If you've never experienced mornings with them, then you cannot fully appreciate their value.

The sunlight is blocked out, the warmth of the darkness allows those few minutes longer of sleep, and the illusion of night cascades through the room, well into the daylight hours.

I've lived here seven weeks and I *still* get surprised *every* morning when I open my bedroom door and have to squint. It's light outside?! Really? But my world was so dark – who knew that light existed outside those four walls…?

Isn't that just like life?

We become trapped within the walls of our pain, regret, bitterness, unforgiveness, hurt or shame, so we cannot see any light loitering outside our world.

There are seasons of darkness we encounter, which truly *are* dark. They are the seasons of grief, rejection and deep hurt, which etch lines into our life stories that time won't erase, but grace will cover. But I'm not speaking about those seasons.

I am talking about the areas of our lives where we have allowed the past to control our present and what 'should have been' to taint what now is.

And if we do not open the curtains of our unbelief to the warmth of God's grace, we will allow that part of our heart to remain in the dark, slowly losing the air of life – like a punctured tyre that flattens over time under use, without repair.

And this, my friend, is most definitely *not* God's will for your life…

Think about those areas of unbelief in your life – where do you find it most difficult to trust God? Why? Ask the Holy Spirit to begin gently pulling away the curtain of unbelief, allowing the light of grace and truth to shine directly into your situation. Spend a few minutes resting and picturing God intricately involved in your situation, wanting your best, and working all things together for good.

Tuesday

Last week we looked at trust, acceptance and mentoring, all in relation to stepping forward into influencing others on this journey.

This week I want us to begin envisioning 'what could be', if we seek risk over reward and impression over impressive.

We all love praise.

I don't know anyone who would say they dislike encouragement – even people who say they don't like to be recognised, prefer it to being slandered.

Deep down we are like children in search of acceptance and approval. We long to know that we've done a job well, and the appreciation of others often is the motivating factor to persevere through conflict we would prefer avoiding.

Saul, before he became Paul, enjoyed recognition. We can imagine him standing above Stephen as he was stoned (Acts 7:54–8:1), with a look of self-content, pride and arrogance for his job well done – another Christian silenced for their blasphemy! Saul was concerned with status (Phil. 3:4–6) and revelled in his intelligence.

But after one encounter with God on the road to Damascus, he was a changed man. He now says, 'But whatever were gains to me

I now consider loss for the sake of Christ' (Phil. 3:7). In other words, what previously impressed him, now held no interest for him. His, and our, only interest should be knowing Christ and seeing His name made famous.

How did Paul achieve this?

One way is found a few verses later, where it says:

> 'But one thing I do: Forgetting what is behind and straining toward what is ahead, I press on toward the goal to win the prize for which God has called me heavenward in Christ Jesus.' (Phil. 3:13–14)

Paul knew that remembering what was done on the cross for him and the future glory, which awaited him, were paramount to maintaining spiritual focus and integrity.

What do you need to remember... in order to forget?

....

....

....

Spend a few minutes meditating on the cross, its implications, and the fact we are seated 'in the heavenly realms in Christ' (Eph. 2:6).

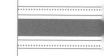

Wednesday

Morning always comes.

Regardless of how dark the night looks…
morning always comes.

There is something comforting about those words.

Morning symbolises new beginnings, a fresh start, light breaking
through the darkness and renewed hope to try again.

What confidence has morning brought you today?

To help others, we must give from a place of grace and not need.
Our needs are met by God (see Phil. 4:19), freeing us to give out of
the grace we have received.

Let morning meet your needs with the knowledge that God sees
you, hears you and knows the deepest longing of your heart. He
is for you, not against you (Rom. 8:31) and you can trust Him to
provide, freeing you to give generously to others who are in a
place of darkness or confusion today.

Read those last two sentences again – let the truth sink in…

Write down your thoughts on trusting God with your future – what scares you about this? Is there anything you struggle to release to Him?

. . . .

. . . .

. . . .

Now is the time to risk trusting His grace. If you are holding something that needs to be let go, write it on a separate piece of paper – and hand it up to Him. Then discard the paper somehow – burn it, tear it up, or put it in the recycleing bin, showing that you've left it in the immensely capable hands of the Creator. Score through your writing above and make a note of the date you surrendered your fears to Him.

Thursday

L ast week we mentioned Moses mentoring Joshua, and how he helped Joshua go from helper to leader, by giving him an opportunity.

This week we look at the second way Moses mentored, which is *Moses illustrated devotion.*

In Exodus 33:11 it says that Moses spoke to God face-to-face, and then left the tent… whilst Joshua remained. Moses was a man who sought God diligently, refusing to move unless God's presence came with them (Exod. 33:15), and Moses was not threatened when Joshua stayed behind – for more one-on-one time with God – because Moses understood that relationship was what would sustain Joshua in the future. Moses knew that he would not always be there, so he needed to continually demonstrate and perpetuate Joshua's dependence on God as El Shaddai.

El Shaddai means 'All-Sufficient One'.

'While Elohim is the God who creates, in the name "Shaddai", God reveals Himself as the God who compels nature to do what is contrary to itself. He is able to triumph over every obstacle and all opposition; He is able to subdue all things to Himself.'*

I love that.

As leaders we *must* find our sufficiency and strength in God. Anything less is self-dependence and will eventually lead to burnout, pride or both.

Never underestimate your time alone with God.

And never underestimate sharing your love of God and His Word with those around you – make them hungry for what you have discovered!

Who around you can be influenced by your love for the Word? By your prayer life? By your love for God, the Church and serving? Are you actively looking for ways to share this?

Write out the names of individuals who you are specifically hoping to encourage and help disciple, as Moses did for Joshua. If you don't know who, pray and ask the Holy Spirit to reveal to you at least one person.

....

....

....

Now purposefully invite that person into your world (if they agree to it), letting them learn from your time with God, assisting you in your serving and giving you the opportunity to speak life into their hopes and dreams.

*www.myredeemerlives.com/namesofgod/el-shaddai.html

143

Friday

W e are not here to be impressive, but to make an impression.

Let me quickly add – there is nothing wrong with being impressive! We are to strive for excellence in all we do, but being impressive should not be the main goal.

When being impressive overtakes leaving an impression, we have got our priorities confused.

Impressive is an impact which draws attention to ourselves; an impression is a legacy whose benefits go beyond our life's borders.

Are there any areas in your life where you are trying to be impressive, over leaving an impression?

'For I resolved to know nothing while I was with you except Jesus Christ and him crucified. I came to you in weakness with great fear and trembling. My message and my preaching were not with wise and persuasive words, but with a demonstration of the Spirit's power, so that your faith might not rest on human wisdom, but on God's power.' (1 Cor. 2:2–5)

The apostle Paul was one of the most educated men in that time, yet after encountering Christ he realised the power of singular focus.

To mentor others and lead them well, we must have this same focus.

In which ways do you seek to impress, rather than leave an impression?

....

....

....

Spend some time praying for the one(s) you want to mentor – even if you haven't asked them yet. Pray for their spiritual journeys, and ask the Lord for ways you can encourage them to grow stronger and go further…

Monday

We're not ready – but He is.

'God's Spirit touches our spirits and confirms who we really are. We know who he is, and we know who we are: Father and children. And we know we are going to get what's coming to us—an unbelievable inheritance! We go through exactly what Christ goes through. If we go through the hard times with him, then we're certainly going to go through the good times with him!'

(Rom. 8:15–17, *The Message*)

Any season of advancement and promotion in my life has found me wanting, feeling ill-equipped and suddenly lacking in knowledge.

Most parents feel this way the moment they hold their newborn, knowing the little life is fully dependent on them for survival.

And though most won't admit it, athletes, politicians and business leaders fiercely battle fears of failure when promoted to the next level.

We may want the podium, but we fear the race.

'I will go before you and will level the mountains; I will break down gates of bronze and cut through bars of iron. I will give you hidden treasures, riches stored in secret places, so that you may know that I am the LORD, the God of Israel, who summons you by name.' (Isa. 45:2–3)

He knows your name. He sees your race. He makes a way.

Remember some of the stories we've mentioned so far –
a young girl named Esther wasn't ready to face the king (Esth. 4),
but God was ready to give her favour and save a nation.

An insecure man named Gideon wasn't ready to lead,
nor face, an army (Judg. 6), but God was ready to empower
him for the miraculous.

Jesus, as man, wasn't ready to face a cross (Matt. 26:39), but God,
as Father, was ready to destroy death once and for all.

In His readiness, we are made ready.

You may not feel ready for the season in front of you, but He is.

He is ready to break down barriers, unlock possibilities, release
favour and make a way. The enemy cannot stop Him, your fears do
not faze Him and time does not limit Him.

It is not too late, nor is it too early; now is the season and you are
the person for this next assignment.

Esther, Gideon and even Jesus did not especially feel 'ready' for what they faced, but all of them completed their assignment, experiencing victory on the other side.

You may see the race, but God sees the podium.

And for that reason He knows… you *are* ready.

Take a few minutes to think about your life currently. Is there a recent promotion you've been given, new ministry, change in circumstances, or new life season you've entered recently? What lessons from your past have you learned that will help you face the potentially daunting aspects of your future?

. . . .

. . . .

. . . .

Tuesday

R egardless of what has happened in the past, our future rests in God's hands of love and He is capable of redeeming time and repairing breaches.

What has happened in our past, whether good or bad, is *experience* – it can be used to help not only ourselves, but others as well.

It is easy to become intensely focused on our own journeys, at the expense of investing in others.

We may think once our lives have more stability, greater experience and increased victories, then we have something to give. It could not be further from the truth.

Yes, we must learn to teach. Having experiences gives you *experience*. There are few things more frustrating than listening to someone pontificate 'wisdom' they have not gained, simply for their own self-interest.

But more often than not, women tend to operate out of insecurity and a devaluing of their own worth, at the expense of the impact they could have had.

You may not understand some of life's chapters, nor may you feel equipped to help write the stories for another, but God knows you are both equipped and ready for what He is asking of you.

Think of those who have greatly impacted you by sharing their experiences – in which areas were you impacted? And why did their sharing particularly affect you?

....

....

....

Use this as a springboard and as inspiration to look for others who would benefit from your insight and encouragement.

With this in mind, what are some experiences you have had, which you could use to teach others? For example, grief, joys, education, obstacles overcome, fears you are facing, mindsets you have changed, spiritual lessons learned.

....

....

....

'**G**ive me six hours to chop down a tree and I will spend the first four sharpening the axe.' – Abraham Lincoln

We tend to fall into one camp or the other: always preparing and too afraid to risk or rarely preparing and making it up as we go!

Preparation cannot be undervalued, nor should it be overused.

Life has prepared you for who you are called to mentor in this season. As mentioned in the week before last, if you are old enough to read these words, you have experience enough to help *someone*.

And we must proactively be looking for that person(s), praying into their future and encouraging their success. Otherwise, we risk getting self-focused, issue consumed and fear driven.

At the same time, never underestimate the preparation you have had, or will have, to influence others. If you feel on the sidelines right now, don't bemoan the fact, embrace the opportunity. You have more time to spend with the Lord, getting filled with what you will one day share!

In what ways do you feel the Lord is preparing you right now?

. . . .

. . . .

. . . .

. . . .

In what ways have you seen Him prepare you in the past for the areas in which you now find yourself giving, serving and mentoring?

. . . .

. . . .

. . . .

. . . .

Thursday

Over the last two weeks, we have mentioned Moses mentoring Joshua. The first week looked at how Moses gave Joshua *opportunity*, and the second week looked at how Moses illustrated *devotion*.

This week we look at the third way: *Moses prepared him as a successor.*

Now read Deuteronomy 31:1–8; 34:9.

Moses clearly had prepared Joshua to lead once he had died. Moses, one of the greatest leaders to have lived, knew that without a successor he had not succeeded.

In a similar way, Jesus equipped Peter only days before the resurrection (John 21:15–22).

In both instances, the leader endorsed the successor in front of the followers.

Belief in those we lead can never be underestimated. They need to hear your praise, know your support, and see your confidence in their abilities. Anything less breeds insecurity and allows seeds of doubt.

In the years prior to Moses' death, Moses allowed Joshua into his world: trusting him in battle, modelling for him an intimate relationship with God, letting him lead under his leadership and making a way for his promotion.

It somewhat amazes me that as a warrior, and with all of that support, Joshua was *still* afraid to lead when it finally became his responsibility (Josh. 1:6–7,9).

We cannot be someone's confidence, but we can intentionally seed *into* their confidence. This requires seeing what could be instead of what is, believing our ceiling will become their floor.

Who are you preparing to go beyond your reach? How are you preparing them, encouraging them and supporting them?

....

....

....

Father God, our lives are meant to exceed our breaths. So I pray now that You will show me who I can mentor, which person in my life can use my encouragement, and where You want me to put my focus in this season. I pray for eyes to see, opportunities to impact and divine appointments to encounter. Thank You that we are part of a larger family and greater vision, each playing a part in Your kingdom plan. Help me play my part to the fullest, I pray. Amen.

Friday

As mentioned previously, there is no success without a successor.

A successor is not something to be taken lightly and the relationship often has the fingerprints of God dusted across its connection and journey. It won't happen without effort, and at times can take years of investment. The weightier the responsibility, the greater the attention to successorship should be taken.

But when speaking of a successor, I'm not only talking about the next president of a corporation or pastor of a church. Taking on a Bible study, mentoring younger women, risking a new business venture, leading a student union – all of these can need successorship.

As in life we find what we look for and see what we search out, I want to challenge us at the end of this journey to seek one in whom we can *invest*. It may take a year of prayer before the right person comes along, or you may know who they are already. Don't go into it lightly, but do go into it intentionally.

Know what you have to give, get an idea of what you want to see, and be prepared to sacrifice on the journey until arrival.

Don't give up if you've tried once or twice and it hasn't worked out. Try again. There are plenty of people who need encouragement, love, support and wisdom.

Give out of plenty and not out of need.

Ensure you are being ministered to, spending time in His beautiful presence, so that your spirit is strengthened and heart is full.

But always – always – keep your eyes open and alert to one who needs what you have to give, can learn from what you have endured and is gifted to fly where you have only walked.

In this season of your life (as a mum, employee, employer, grandparent, student, daughter), who has God placed around you that you could – overtly or subtly – mentor?

What is your next step in making a successorship reality?

....

....

....

Loving Father, thank You for the time we have spent in Your presence. Thank You for the gifts of sisterhood, friendship, mentoring and family. You are so wise in connecting our purposes with those of others, showing us that we need each other, as we need You. Lead us to the right people. Create divine relationships in the next few months. Open doors we could not see previously. And let us have unlimited, whole, life-giving relationships with You and one another, leaving a legacy for the next generation to stand upon and reach further than we ever could. I thank You. And... I love You. Amen.

Notes

More devotional journals from

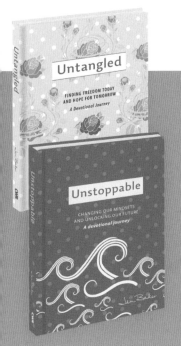

God is good. He has good plans for you.

Fear and regrets can often hold us back. Learn how to overcome such challenges by exploring different 'Freedom from…' themes and delve into a transformative time with God.

ISBN: 978-1-85345-917-7

Learn how to think like the child of God that you are!

What we believe affects every area of our lives. So how can we meditate on God's Word until His truth becomes our belief?

ISBN: 978-1-78259-754-4

Unshakeable Confidence

Looking back over her own experiences, Jen Baker explores how we can walk tall as women of Christ.

ISBN: 978-1-78259-840-4

Inspiring Women Every Day

Inspiring Women Every Day is written by women, for women, and provides biblical and life-applicable inspiration, insight and encouragement for women of all ages.

Published bimonthly. Available as single issues and as a one-year subscription.

Find out more at cwr.org.uk/inspiringwomen

Courses and events

Waverley Abbey College

Publishing and media

Conference facilities

Transforming lives

CWR's vision is to enable people to experience personal transformation through applying God's Word to their lives and relationships.

Our Bible-based training and resources help people around the world to:
• Grow in their walk with God
• Understand and apply Scripture to their lives
• Resource themselves and their church
• Develop pastoral care and counselling skills
• Train for leadership
• Strengthen relationships, marriage and family life and much more.

Our insightful writers provide daily Bible reading notes and other resources for all ages, and our experienced course designers and presenters have gained an international reputation for excellence and effectiveness.

CWR's Training and Conference Centre in Surrey, England, provides excellent facilities in an idyllic setting – ideal for both learning and spiritual refreshment.

CWR Applying God's Word
to everyday life and relationships

CWR, Waverley Abbey House,
Waverley Lane, Farnham,
Surrey GU9 8EP, UK

Telephone: **+44 (0)1252 784700**
Email: info@cwr.org.uk
Website: cwr.org.uk

Registered Charity No. 294387
Company Registration No. 1990308